Happy Husband
Happy Life

By Burks & Davis

Copyright © 2015 Burks & Davis

ISBN: 0692573569
ISBN-13: 978-0692573563

Legal Notice

No part of this book may be reproduced or transmitted in any form whatsoever, electronic or mechanical, including photocopying, recording or by any informational storage or retrieval system without express writer, dated and signed permission from the author.

The information presented herein represents the view of the authors as of the date of publication. Because of the rate with which conditions change, the authors reserve the right to alter and update their opinion based on the new conditions. The report is for informational purposes only.

While every attempt has been made to verify the information provided in this book, neither the authors nor their affiliates/partners assume any responsibility for errors, inaccuracies or omissions.

Contents

Contents 3
Disclaimer 4
The Honest Truth 5
A Woman's Guide 7
Something Doesn't Seem Right..............................8
False Platforms...10
We Can't Be 50/50...14
You're In Love With Lies 16
Ms. Independent...18
Can't Turn A Hoe Into A Housewife 20
Mrs. Right 22
Men Are To Blame 24
Nice Guys Finish Last..26
A Man's Guide...29
Protect Your Investment 36
Mr. Right..38
Man in the Mirror 41
Enough is enough 42
Improve Yourself for Yourself.............................44
    Step 1: Be Honest with Yourself 44
    Step 2: Cut Ties 44
    Step 3: Try Harder 46
    Step 4: Forgive the Forgotten 46
In Closing 48

Disclaimer

First off, a small disclaimer, this book is for both women and men. Secondly, this book was created to show men and women what's right and wrong about the dynamics of today's relationships. Now a little bit about what the book is not. This book is not about bashing women and this book is definitely not an "all men are great" type of book. It's not a book to teach you how to get what you want from a man or your husband but it will show you how to keep your husband or obtain one. It's not to teach you how to pick up women but it will show you how to keep your woman more than satisfied and happy. It's truly a simplistic relationship guide. Peruse and apply the information and examples given from the book and your marriage or relationship will see a tremendous change "for better or for worse".

The Honest Truth

Men and women have different perspectives on what entails a happy relationship. Women tend to qualify what's good for a relationship based on what's good for them. When a woman establishes "those things", she will then sell a man on the same ideas to qualify or disqualify them as an eligible mate. Even when a woman is already married, she will use those same techniques on her spouse to convince him that she's the ideal catch. Women have to learn that they should sell what men are buying instead of selling what they find most valuable. Men may not be looking for those certain qualities in a woman but if that woman thinks she's strong in a certain area or she likes specific things about herself, then men should too. Men don't be fooled, women will never announce a quality that they're looking for in a man that they don't already think they have. So men, pay attention to what women say they're looking for because it will give you a head start into the type of woman you're dealing with and the type of relationship you have to look forward to.

As far as men go, men don't take ownership today. Men have to realize that they're most vital to a woman's mental success. Men have to accept that they're the leaders and that they have to stop acting foolish about everything when it involves a relationship or a woman. Playing with a woman's emotions and only trying to have sex with women is nothing more than low class and it also backfires. Men don't realize that this creates hell for them and it creates hell for the next man. Men have to grow up and accept the responsibility of the relationship which calls for men to take on various roles for a woman. So without further ado, let's set things back in order.

A Woman's Guide

As promised, this is a simple book to read so it was necessary to provide women with a checklist, check point, reference or whatever you want to call it at the beginning of the book. This is so when you're going through the material, you can come back and ask yourself, "Is this me" or "Am I these things"? If you're going to be in a successful relationship, you need to be able to do all 4 of the following items effortlessly:

1. You need to be able to LISTEN
2. You should know how to be SUBMISSIVE
3. You have to be willing to be CONTROLLABLE
4. You have to be OBEDIENT

There is no negotiating with the listing given above. If those 4 rules rubbed you the wrong way, well that's good. Congratulations! That means you have the opportunity to learn. The book will show you how to be a positive woman and how to have a successful relationship. On the other hand, if those 4 rules didn't bother you, and I mean didn't bother you at all, congratulations, you're probably in a successful relationship already and this book will be no more than a good read and refresher for you. It's truly a win/win for all women.

Something Doesn't Seem Right

So let's jump right into it. Let's get into why so many relationships are defeated before they even begin. Women, it's just that simple. All relationships fail because of the women involved, directly or indirectly and if you continue reading you'll soon agree and find out why.

Women today are screwed. Social media, mixed with _____ friends (friends has a _____ in front of it because you should insert what type of friends you have in the blank space provided. It could be nosey, mean, stupid, worrisome, ugly, pretty, broke, rich or anything you like can be inserted because it doesn't matter) accompanied by dishonest men, with years of bad habits picked up from their scorned mothers or other scorned relatives is just a recipe for disaster. With that alone you should already be thinking well maybe women are the reason for this debacle in today's relationships.

Social media and your _____ friends carry around the same weight of importance. Honestly, social media may have the edge over friends today. You know, social media can dictate how a woman acts or reacts in her own relationship from what she may have read or seen from a complete stranger. She doesn't even have to know the person but if that woman can relate to those comments posted, she will latch onto those comments and treat them as validation or a point of reference to endorse her emotions and feelings. In reality, social media is full of blogs, vlogs, tweets and memes created by people who either are scorned and angry or attempting to gain followers. Most times people will say what they think you want to hear in order to get what they want. Friends and social media tend to have much more control over women because of how much weight another woman's opinion tends to carry. (--------)It's really that simple. Women care about what other women think. It doesn't matter how ridiculous it is or what the other woman may be saying, women will give attention to it. Without the proper guidance, those awful impressions will stick and become law. Those impressions then spawn insecurities and those insecurities then lead to fear of judgment and in general the source of that judgment is other women. These are just the friends we're talking about. Those friends in addition to what strangers may think of you on Facebook, Twitter, or Instagram will produce chaos. Can you see how complicated this becomes for you and your relationship when you're living your life based on what all these other people may think of you? It's hard to put that level of complication into words but you get it. It's best to focus entirely on your relationship and not worry about the opinions of others with misleading views and assessments that don't have a clue about anything. It becomes the blind leading the blind and every woman thinks they have 20/20 vision when it comes to a relationship.

False Platforms

Something I've noticed over the years with being in and out of relationships and around different types of women is how women create or listen to misleading advice. In the beginning of new relationships, women tell other women all the time, "in order to get a man, you need to know how to cook, you better take care of those toes and nails, you need to make sure your makeup is done, you better make sure you wear matching panties and bras, get your hair done, etc, etc, you better, you better, you better". Listen, this is very bad advice and it's even worse to think that it's true. You have to realize that when women give you this advice they don't ever say anything about the guy. This is a false platform that keeps women fixated on them and in return it makes them feel like they are the only important person in the relationship. See it doesn't take much to get your hair and nails done, cook, and dress yourself accordingly but honestly you should already be doing those things for yourself. Trust that I'm not saying guys are more important but if you're in a relationship with a woman and she's first priority that relationship will fail. It'll fail because that woman will never listen or be happy. We'll get into why later when we introduce you to the "nice guys".

A popular example of a false platform that's constantly used is "we're not compatible". "We're just not compatible" is an escape phrase that everyone uses in their relationship at one time or another. The expression is solely used to convey unhappiness. Sometimes men and women even allow compatibility to be the determining factor when deciding if a relationship will last or fail. Compatibility is a myth that doesn't exist and it doesn't need to exist in order to have a successful relationship. Let's define what compatibility is. Compatibility is defined as being capable of existing or living together in harmony. That's compatibility; it's a result of respect. Compatibility does not mean you have to like what your spouse or significant other likes. Compatibility is not doing the same activities that your spouse or significant other would want to do. Compatibility is not liking the same music, food, destinations, political parties, or even having the same religious beliefs. As compatibility is defined, it's all about feeling, harmony and co-existence. You should not believe you have to be with someone like you or closely like you in order to have peace, harmony and happiness. If you think about it, a man and a woman typically - doesn't like doing what the other one likes. Now I'm not saying that men and women can't enjoy the same activities but there shouldn't be any warning flags if a man and a woman isn't excited about each other's extracurricular activities. For example, a man may want to go out to a bar and watch boxing all night, his woman probably wouldn't want to do that. As a woman, you may want to go on an all day shopping spree with your girlfriends, get your nails done and talk about the latest celebrity news, your man isn't likely to be onboard with that or look forward to that day. But it's okay to embrace those differences. It's those differences that make us more attractive to one another. Those differences give us the possibility for expanding our own views, knowledge, and interest. So the next time you hear or mention this saying "we're not compatible", ask yourself or your spouse "what's making us unhappy", then fix it.

Another distorted idea that women believe is that they have control over a man and their relationship. The "men do what their women allow them to" phrase is a misleading concoction of lies and garbage. Men are going to do what they want to do and you "allowing it" are more bogus thoughts that women grasp on in order to feel like they have some type of control. Women can't control a man and women can't be in control of a relationship. It goes back to women not knowing what they want. Think about it. Guys, how many times have you thought about getting something to eat and you ask, "Where do you want to go to babe?" and she responds "I don't know". Men, women want you to lead. It's up to you to make decisions and stand by them, because if you don't, understand what happens next. You will suggest somewhere and she will say "I don't want that", "I don't like that" and the game will continue as you attempt to create happiness for her, over and over again. Women don't know what they want; they just want to be led. As the leader, you don't make suggestions, you give answers. So if you give a person control and they have no direction or they don't know what to do with the responsibility that you've given them, it's not going to end well. If you were a millionaire, you wouldn't give your ten year old $100,000 would you? So if you're a man, why would you give your woman the responsibility to build and lead a successful relationship? Women are unfit to do so because they are such emotional people. As it would be wrong to think a ten year old would make a sound decision with $100,000, it's also wrong for a man to think a woman can design a sound relationship by being the leader. Women are great at needing but not so great at being needed. If you put that kind of pressure on a woman to lead, she may handle it well for a period of time but there will come a time that she looks at you in disgust. She will ask herself "Why am I taking care of this grown man?" A woman with that type of control will become stressed out with you and that control will feel unnatural for her. How can she feel like a woman when she's busy playing the role of a man and when she's having to be everything that she wants you to be. Men have to take control of their position and women have to be honest with them. Women should stop wanting control and become the supporter of the relationship so the balance can become or remain healthy but men you have to lead by example.

We Can't Be 50/50

Women love the idea that they are equal to men and that they share the same responsibilities evenly in the relationship. People say this so quickly that they never take the time to analyze this concept. How is it even possible for a man and a woman to be equal in a relationship? Most times, women are not splitting half of the responsibilities and even if they are, the value of a man's responsibilities always outweighs the woman's responsibilities. Please don't misunderstand what I am saying. What women contribute is very important and is needed greatly but men take on more of the responsibilities. Why? Because of the emotional onus of a relationship. Men and women overlook the emotional duties that men have to carry. Being the shoulder to lean on, being the mild-tempered one, being the teacher and leader all count as an additional responsibility. It's actually a huge responsibility in itself. So it can't be equal between men and women because women are not going to perform those tasks. They would not be able to handle it. You have to understand roles and you have to have an appreciation for your role and its value. You shouldn't feel like it has to be equal in order to carry your weight in the relationship. You have to commit to your set of responsibilities in your relationship. To say you're in an equal relationship or that you're pursuing one is just another way of avoiding submission and not accepting a man as the leader. This is the wrong mindset and it automatically gets your relationship off on the wrong track. The funny thing about being equal in the relationship is women watch television and movies and every relationship they admire are those that show a man being a strong man, a man in control and a man that's taking care of everything. Those relationships are not equal but that's what women are infatuated with. So what is it that you really want? These things look attractive in Hollywood but in real life you won't allow yourself the same types of relationships.

You're In Love With Lies

Let's just go ahead and admit to this. As women, you love being lied to. The truth just doesn't sound as good as a lie. The lies build you up and allow you to remain in a safe zone. It protects you from all of your fears and insecurities. Lies work. They work because you would rather hear them than the truth. Lies have become the normalcy in your life. When this happens, even the truth starts to feel like a lie to you. As a matter of fact, lies are probably so prominent in your life that when you hear the truth, you can dismiss it by going elsewhere and attaining another lie to make yourself feel better. Women are the first to say they want an honest man but can't always handle honesty. It's understandable because your whole life you're pretty much lied to by everybody. You're lied to by countless guys trying to sleep with you. You're lied to by your parents telling you, "you can be anything you want to be", that "you don't need a man" or that "you're beautiful", so in a sense, women just don't know any better. They rather be lied to because again that's what they're use to. Women make up excuses like, "oh, he just wasn't the right one" or "I just haven't met that special guy" or "they're not any good guys out there" or "there's someone for everyone", which are all forms of fabrication. Women don't want to accept the truth. Women respect the men that are telling them everything they want to hear because that's what life has conditioned them to accept. This is why I state women don't know what they want, they want honesty but don't know how to receive it when it's given. When a person is honest, it's always too harsh, when a person lies; it just is what it is.

It's just normal. So an example, if I tell a girl that she's not beautiful but average looking and that she would be able to have a much happier relationship or marriage if she respected her husband more and didn't talk as much, I would pretty much look like an asshole. But if a smooth criminal told her she was beautiful and she didn't need to change herself because nothing is wrong and "your guy just doesn't get you", he would look like Prince Charming. The mental equilibrium of a woman is constantly tainted by lies. What women are fighting for doesn't even exist. Women seek and respect honesty but they encourage and reward dishonest behavior. Women have to be rewired and for that rewiring to take place, women have to be able to abide by the 4 laws in the "Woman's Guide" so that the leader who is your "right guy", can successfully undo the wrong doing and complete the rewiring.

Remember a woman's truth is based on her current mind state. Due to the constant change in emotions, a woman will be very fickle in what she sees as true. So men must remain consistent and patient at all times. What women believe may change day to day but men you can't be thrown off by that. Continue to stay focused so you can guide that woman through her emotions and help her be the best version of herself possible, because if you don't, it will only reinforce what she's been taught her entire life and it will only make it more difficult for you, to break a self-reliant thinker.

Ms. Independent

Let's talk about the independent woman, "Ms. Independent". This has to be one of the most ridiculous misconceptions that society has implanted in men and women. The whole mentality of a woman thinking she doesn't need a man is nothing more than an abomination. In order to survive, pro-create or be successful, you need more than yourself. Our entire childhood, we are dependent upon people. We depend on certain individuals to take care of us, clothe us and to feed us. Even when we are teenagers, we continue to be dependent upon people. Why is it when women get out of college or they reach their early twenties, everything that was learned from an early age about being dependent is thrown out the window and everything that was taught to them is replaced by "I'm an independent woman". Why does this mindset set in? I can tell you. It's because of the horrible influences of other broken women. We have all heard the saying "one rotten apple spoils the bunch" this statement is true indeed. Independency has lost the context of what it really means today because it's taken to be a literal concept. You will always require an undeniable level of dependency from someone or something to survive and become successful. Yes, you want to be able to function independently but you must understand that because you're capable of doing most things on your own, it doesn't mean that doing it yourself or by yourself will be the most efficient way. For example, you may have some co-workers that are better suited to handle some job-related task-. Wouldn't it make more sense to have your co-workers do them, do them quickly and correctly the first time, so you won't have to struggle with it as much? Now that's logical enough and simple enough to understand. Now apply this thought process to your relationship. Just because you may not "need" a man to lead you does not mean having a man lead you isn't the more efficient way. By no means is it being suggested that you become helpless and confide all in one man but you should abandon the idea of "no need for anyone but myself" and abandon the idea of independency. Obviously this concept doesn't exist. Women often say they're independent to imply that they don't need a man. To imply that you don't need a man is to deny your own femininity. Feminine energy is drawn to masculine energy and masculine energy is drawn to feminine energy in order to create balance. Its balance that we all yearn to have and to deny it is only denying your true self. So ladies let's end the chapter on this regarding "independence", if you want to be independent, make sure your attempts for independency are in the world like at your job or with your peers but not in your relationships. Because men, an independent woman will never remove herself out the equation, it will always be about her and you'll never be able to build a successful unified foundation.

Can't Turn A Hoe Into A Housewife

We need to briefly discuss the difference between a hoe and a housewife. It's easy to distinguish the two. A hoe is a woman you can't control and a housewife is someone you can. Please understand that any housewife can be a hoe and any hoe can be a housewife. It's all about a woman's mental psyche. Honestly, most women are hoes until they're trained to think and do better. A housewife is someone you can work with and can deal with on a day to day basis. There's no working with hoes. Hoes have the mindset of an independent woman and an independent mindset in a relationship equals disaster. It falls right in line with a Woman's Guide. A housewife will be willing to listen, be submissive, controllable and obedient. Hoes will only carry one or two of those traits, so don't be fooled. If there's a woman that exhibits all of these traits, still give yourself time before you take it to the next level. Many hoes will trick you and pretend for a while to get what they want. If you don't give in to their demands, they will eventually faze themselves out because the work will be too difficult to keep up with and her actions will show you an "independent woman". When she starts showing signs of this, you should realize this woman isn't for you and that you would only be wasting your time with her because this woman has no intentions of being "Mrs. Right". But let me make this clear, hoes aren't women who sleep around. Hoes are women that are mentally incapable of controlling themselves. Hoes make it impossible for you to construct something serious. Be careful when dealing with hoes and if you don't take anything away from this chapter please remember this, there is no "I" in team nor house, so when you take "us" out of house, you're only left with a hoe. Read it again, you'll get it.

Mrs. Right

Most men today can't tell a good woman from a bad one. Men today get confused with lust for love. All men are pretty much in love with the same woman, which is the woman that's very beautiful, the woman that's very successful, the woman with the outstanding body, or your latest celebrity. Men and woman have the idea that everyone should already be put together. Put together for them before they even make an investment into a relationship with a person. This is a mistake, especially on the man's behalf. There is no perfect person sitting around waiting to find you. This beautiful, successful woman with the outstanding body will still require a certain amount of effort on your part to create a happy relationship. As the leaders in the household and the relationship, you have to understand that most women are going to need guidance, supported by a man's patience, and a willingness to teach a woman how to be happy. With that being said, before a man makes an investment into any woman, he should realize if that woman will be willing to be a team player or not. What do I mean by "team player"? I mean a woman that's willing to listen even when she doesn't want to. A woman that's paying attention even when she's most upset. Small gestures like this are big deals in a relationship. Just having a woman who shows you that little bit of respect and shows that willingness to take on her role is a huge difference. It's the difference between having someone on your side and someone that's opposing you. Where most men go wrong today, they make lucrative judgments off a woman's appearance that ends up costing a hefty price and a heck of a lot of wasted time. Let's give you an example of how this correlates in today's workforce. You would never promote an employee to a position of power within your company if that employee didn't see your company's vision. So if they started in the mailroom and they were not a productive worker or didn't share the company's goals, you would leave them in the mailroom or fire them. See people today give too many promotions to employees that barely even deserve a job. Employees start wanting more and start working less. Why would you do more for them when they're undeserving? So why even get in a relationship with someone that doesn't hold your word and opinion in high regard? Why would you attach yourself to a person that doesn't respect you or the relationship? Why would you get into a relationship with someone that doesn't want to get married but marriage is one of your goals? You already know how it's going to be from the beginning. See I'm not talking about so-called "compatibility" like people refer to; I'm talking about unity, honesty and respect. Stop promoting unfit people to positions in your life that don't share the same goals and visions.

Men Are To Blame

Today, women are solely responsible for the demise of the relationship. We have to ask ourselves though, who should we blame for the demise of women. The woman you're with is rarely at fault when it comes to her behavior. Women are doing what they've learned over time and men are at fault when they allow it to happen. If you are with a woman you're invested in, men, you have to learn how to correct bad behaviors. See a woman is a reflection of the influences in her life but over time she will eventually take on the man's personality that she's with. A fine distinction. Think about it like this, a supervisor or manager is at fault if a team member doesn't succeed. That supervisor is responsible for grooming and coaching those employees. It's not the employees fault if they fail. It's not the employees fault if they do not have clear instructions on what to do. It's not the employees fault if they haven't been given the proper tools to be successful at their job. It would be the supervisor's fault; his job would be to prepare his employees. It's a man's fault if that woman doesn't succeed. He is responsible for grooming and coaching that woman. A supervisor leads by example, they work hard and the employees normally follow. So if you're a bad supervisor, you can't realistically expect your employees to perform at a high level. As this correlates to today's relationships, if you are a woman with an irresponsible man and he's not leading you correctly, you can't take the blame for your actions or thought process. See men can't leave a situation to a woman to figure out on her own because she will only create her own story and in return create hell for him. As the leader, you should always make sure that you're honest, straight-forward and clear-cut in direction so that a woman won't create lies that will end up needing more time and conversation to fix. You may think the work can be avoided and that the hard conversations will go away but it won't, they will manifest. It's always best to address situations as they arise in the relationship because you're then being proactive and not reactive to problems. Good leadership isn't good if you're picking and choosing the moments to be a good communicator or be open and honest. You can't avoid problems by being a "nice guy" because you're afraid of upsetting a women or potentially losing her.

Nice Guys Finish Last

Since women are emotional creatures their mindset will change often. Therefore if you are a man trying to entertain that, you will always be playing catch up and you will always lose. You will always remain in the friend zone or be known as the "lame guy" with that woman. That goes hand in hand with the statement, "nice guys finish last". The nice guy is the guy always doing what is asked of him and he is always listening to the confusing rhetoric of a woman. He will go to work night and day to pay for that engagement ring and give that woman everything her heart desires, all the while, the Smooth Criminal down the street is coming into his home, dominating his woman in every aspect. Men, you have to learn how to become men. The "right guy" not the "nice guy" will give a woman everything she needs but not all that she wants. All that means is that you have to become leaders.

Let's objectively look at an example of what "nice guys" do that put them behind. "Nice guys" hold purses. Before, we take a look at that example, men, don't ever hold a purse again and if you are holding purses, stop, like right now. See women want a masculine man but doesn't know what it takes to be one. Women, if you make or allow a man to carry a purse then you're lessening his manhood in your eyes subconsciously. Both men and women don't understand that when a man carries a purse it turns him into something that a woman is not attracted to, a weak man. A purse isn't an item a man neither needs nor was it created for him. Now holding a purse may seem like a small thing but if you add a bunch of small things like this up, a woman will eventually become less attracted to you, not respect you as much and desire other men because your masculinity has been taken away. The world has made holding a purse the gentlemanly thing to do and it's not. This goes back to women thinking they know what they want but really not knowing at all. Women never want the nice guy; it just looks good and sounds good on paper. Now look at this, in one of the old Superman movies, Superman gave away his powers to be with Lois Lane. He was in love with this woman and the only way they could be together would be by him giving up his super powers and he did. Now what's funny about the Superman example is Lois Lane loved Superman, not Clark Kent. Because he loved her, he was willing to change who he truly was and become a person that Lois Lane didn't even want to be with. But again, he's Superman and she's just an average woman who thinks she deserves a superhero. Men you have to remember, once you give up your power for a woman she will no longer be attracted to you. Where nice guys go wrong, they let women lead the relationships which result in a man changing himself into a person that women don't even desire. A "pushover". That's when a guy starts to give a woman everything she thinks she wants and the relationship becomes turmoil. The man isn't happy, the woman isn't happy and he can't satisfy the thirst of the woman constantly wanting more. Look, nice guys have to remember and be honest with themselves, the majority of the time they are just stepping stones for other men. Nice guys normally assist women into the arms of men who would just tell them anything. Those are the men you call "Dream Sellers" who truly are the bad guys. "You're perfect just how you are". Dream Sellers. "I'm not like other guys". Dream Sellers. "I can't believe he did you like that, if I was with a woman like you I'd never do that". Dream Sellers. And what's the line they use most "No I don't have a girlfriend". See "Dream Sellers" aren't honest, caring or the "right guy" like most women think. A "Dream Seller" will sell you whatever it is he thinks you might be willing to buy. "Dream Sellers" are to blame for a majority of the scorned women that exist today. Some of you are married to dream sellers and you don't even know it. Take a look at your husbands and ask yourself "What dream did he sell me that he hasn't fulfilled like he said he would"? Now for "Mr. nice guy", look at the disservice you create for women when you let them roam free and you give into their every demand. Women just ask yourself, how many times have you left the nice guy and thought about what your life would be like if you stayed? I can tell you. It would be horrible. It would be horrible because you would get tired of the same old feminine qualities; you would eventually get bored, desire other guys and then want to leave all over again. And that's because you want to be led, you want a man to take control. So men, remain yourself no matter who the woman is and always remain in control of the relationship.

A Man's Guide

Be honest at all times. Stop lying. Stop telling every woman that you meet or the woman that you're currently with, what you think they want to hear. More than likely you're lying, she knows you're lying and no one is happy but everyone deals with it because the two of you are used to each other. It's just a perpetual cycle of misery.

A man's guide is a little more difficult than a women's guide because the man is actually responsible for how the woman acts. Many people don't believe this when I tell them but a man has all the responsibility in the relationship when it comes to training and breaking a woman with bad habits and I'll show you. Example: Everyone should be familiar with Cesar Milan the "The Dog Whisperer". Cesar goes to these dog owners with bad dog's and watch the dog's do whatever the dog does to misbehave. Cesar immediately makes the dog's do whatever it is the owner is trying to do but cannot do. So let's stop right here for a minute and ask ourselves in the example. Who really has the problem when we watch the show? Is it the dog or is it the owner? It's the owner. Cesar trains the owner, not the dog. So to relate this to our guide for men, you teach the leader, which is the man in the relationship, how to lead and let him correct his situation, his "situation" being his woman. Because you can't train a dog how not to be a dog and you definitely can't teach a woman how not to be anything other than a woman. As Cesar shows us, you have to teach the owner how to do things that control the dog based on that dog's nature but the dog is still going to do dog things instinctively, as women alike. The man in the relationship needs to know or needs to be trained on how to control that woman based on her nature and that is exactly what this book does. On a side note, I'm not comparing women to dogs or calling them bitches but you have to admit, it's a good example. Women aren't to blame if they aren't trained properly; it's the man to blame. So the next time you're out in public and you see a woman going off, talking loudly or just acting extra for attention, I guarantee she's either single or the guy she's with is weak and miserable. No training!

Lesson 1: Making your woman happy is a suicide mission. As the title of the book states "Happy Husband – Happy Life", the phrase is such an honest statement and I'm going to prove it. When has a woman ever been with a guy and if he wasn't happy, she was happy?

Exercise 1: Think back hard about this. Can you recall a time when your husband, boyfriend, or whoever was upset about something and the relationship was still good? The relationship continued to progress and everyone still handed out hugs and kisses? You probably can't because it's not going to happen, and if it did happen, you couldn't have been that serious with that person. As a woman, think about it, if you were still happy and your husband, fiancé or whomever wasn't happy but you continued to get things you wanted, were you asking for them? Were you forcing him to do things he didn't genuinely want to do. More than likely the answer is "yes". Trust me, at this point the relationship becomes a job and resentment will surely follow. So does this sound like a healthy relationship to be a part of? Relationships where one person is pretty much miserable but keeps giving into you or giving you things to avoid confrontation. Sounds pretty depressing.

Exercise 2: Think of a time a woman has been completely happy once she's gotten everything she's asked for? No complaints, no fussing, arguing, no nothing? It hasn't happen. You know why? Women again have no clue what they want. Women are emotional creatures, so things they want today, they are not going to want tomorrow. How they feel today, they won't feel the same way tomorrow. Women can love you on Monday, hate you by Thursday and be in love with you again by Saturday. Men, recognize that women are chasing a "moment to moment" happiness. Achieving that happiness is impossible for both them and for the naive guy that believes he can help her obtain it. If you allow your woman or spouse to take you on that rollercoaster of a journey, she will not only succeed but she will look down on you when you're not able to fully achieve this impossible task.

Lesson 2: Keep away from Children (Divide and Conquer). Women tend to act like children. They scream, shout, pout, have temper tantrums, get jealous and sometimes get mad with you for no reason. Men have to have patience at all times and especially if this is your wife or a woman you plan to invest your time with. Most women have bad influences around them in what I like to call a "woman's poison" or they have a past of immature encounters and erroneous information. Men have to become the teachers with no distractions in order to achieve relationship success. Men have to understand in order to teach and empower a woman, you have to create a clean mental notepad for them. In order to create that notepad where a woman will listen and retain information, you have to put some distance between her and those bad influences. Not forever but until that woman is no longer under the influence of stupidity and able to make rational decisions without emotions attached. It's rare that a woman will formulate her own opinion without the help of others which may consist of friends, family or entertainment. It's like a lion and their cub, until that cub grows and can protect itself, it's not let out of the parents sight to roam on its own. The cub wouldn't survive. The same applies to your relationship and your woman regarding her bad influences. Example: You wouldn't want your VP of your company having the same mindset as the cafeteria worker, janitor or mailroom worker. You wouldn't want your VP spending too much time around them. My whole point comes down to this, if your VP wants to spend time with those types of people you have to stop that from happening. Educate your VP on what their role is and then make sure the two of you are moving with unity towards the same goals. You can't have your VP talking about or thinking about what they can do to make the mailroom better. You can't have your VP talking about, what products smell better in the bathroom after speaking to the janitors. Don't get me wrong, it's good to socialize, be friendly and show concern but you can't forget about what your responsibilities are and lose sight of what you're there for. At the end of the day it starts to waste time and eventually you lose sight of the company's vision. At some point you have to prevent your VP from going around people and doing certain things until they are conditioned to dismiss nonsense on their own. You have to see how this is parallel with your relationships. It goes with this old saying "Married women shouldn't be friends with single women" and that is completely true. Unless you're with a woman that is conditioned not to take on those single-minded opinions and ideas, she should not be intermingling with single women. Men, I'm not saying control women. First of all that doesn't work and it will backfire. Everything in a relationship should be about desire. Women should have the desire to be controlled, as she should want you to desire to do things for her but not out of obligation. There's a big difference! We must remember, that you have to divert the bad influences until the woman you're with is willing and able to do so herself. This will be a constant, uphill battle when trying to groom and lead the women that you're invested in.

Lesson 3: Create open Communication. There aren't too many men that can have an honest conversation with the women they're with. Men should realize if they can't be honest and speak openly, not disrespectfully, to the person that's most close to them, then they have already lost. Men have to realize the relationship will fail because you can't lead without successful communication. Example: When is the last time you've told the girl you're with that you find other women attractive? Why can't you do this? Why is this forbidden? Its honesty, it promotes an open, honest forum for communication. It also builds trust. We have to stop letting women dictate the relationship resulting in countless arguments and creating liars out of men. Did you know once you become a "liar" in the relationship, that woman becomes the leader and seizes the control over you and the relationship? At this point they determine the terms of the relationship as well. Women control what's okay for you to think and what's okay for you to say because you fear how she will react to whatever it is you do or say, so you edit yourself. That's total control. Therefore, a lying man can't be the leader because he's attempting to appease a woman's expectations which will result to an unhappy relationship. It all goes back to if you're lying you're not happy. If you're not happy, then the woman you're with will not be happy because your happiness dictates the happiness of your woman and the fulfillment in the relationship. The other saying goes "Happy wife, happy life", right? This implies that the man must make the woman happy in order to have a happy life. Well, how can a man make his woman happy if he is unhappy? Happiness has to start with the man. I challenge every man to go to the woman they're with and express to her how much you're attracted to other women. Not that you want the relationship to end or anything like that but how you are tired of looking at women and trying to hide it. Express how much you want to be honest with her moving forward. Explain how you want to answer the question with a "hell yes" when she asks you "Do you think that girl over there is pretty?" I challenge you all to be open and honest. If you get slapped, that's fine, be patient there's no need to react. If your woman starts to become emotional and cry, that's fine, honesty will bring you all closer together. If your woman is top of the line upset and this creates the destruction of your relationship, that's great as well because if something so minor could end your relationship, she's not the one. You wouldn't want anything cemented like mortgages or children with a person like that. On a side note, if you're a man and you already have children, mortgages and things like that invested with a woman and this type of open communication ends the relationship, be honest, it was going to end either way. Look at it as a favor and recognize you owe us one. Now you can really get started with finding your happiness. People, realize that open forum communication creates a stronger bond and not a weaker one. That open forum will only allow women to trust men more and it will also show them that men can lead the relationship into happiness. So once your woman trusts you, she will then allow you to teach her and groom her so you all can grow together successfully.

Protect Your Investment

One thing men should know when trying to settle down with a woman or if you're already married, is that women are investments. As with all important investments, in order for that investment to grow, you have to contribute to that investment accordingly and you have to keep away wrongdoers. Wrongdoers being anyone who would cause that investment harm. Example: You take $1000 to a financial advisor at the bank and every month he tells you your money is looking good but every month you keep losing $100, at some point you would say, "Sir, you're not helping me and I don't think you really care about my investment. So with that being said, I'm taking my money as far away as I can from you and I will never let you near it again". Now this doesn't mean, you wouldn't trust another advisor with your money but you definitely wouldn't deal with the person who kept affecting your investment negatively. You would also pay closer attention to the next financial advisor and how they handle your investments. This is exactly how you should view your woman. As you would question and protect your money, you need to look at your woman or spouse as the same type of investment and be willing to question and protect her. Just like the first financial advisor, you're going to have people who could care less about you and your relationship. On the other hand, you will have some people that care and respect what you are trying to do. So looking at your woman as being your investment, you have to watch out for the types of advisors she has in her life, aka friends, family and influences, because the "wrong advisors" could turn a good investment bad, quickly.

Mr. Right

Throughout the chapters, you'll see the term used the "right guy". We're going to tell you how to know if you are with the "right guy" or not and it's quite simple. If you respect the guy that you're with and you're willing to do all 4 laws listed in a "woman's guide" for that man then you are with the "right guy". One thing women should realize is that all men are different just like themselves. If a man leads, shows you respect and if he doesn't take advantage of you, while you're executing the 4 laws in a "woman's guide" then ladies there you have it, he's the "right guy". One of the items women will take issue within the 4 laws will be the feeling of weakness. Women have to pay attention though to the "the right guy". The "right guy" will never abuse his power and the "right guy" will never make you feel less or ever view you as a weak person in the process. If you look what entails "Mr. Right", there wasn't anything mentioned about money, compatibility, education, neither looks nor love? All of those things mentioned -play a role in the relationship but none are part of the foundation of true happiness. Ladies, your "right guy" all depends on you and what you're willing to accept so you can be successful with the 4 laws in a "woman's guide". Again, men have the duty of leading the relationship but women truly are the pulse of the relationship. So the exercise for you to do at this point is to ask yourself these five questions:

1. Do I respect this man?
2. Do I listen to this man?

3. Am I submissive to this man?
4. Do I mind giving up control to this man?
5. Can I be obedient with this man?

If you answered "no" to anyone of the questions above, then you're wasting your time in the relationship and you should get out as fast as you can. See what people have forgotten is that relationships are simple. Over the years we have created this stigma within relationships that they're supposed to difficult and that there is always suppose to be a debate with one another. It's not! And let me touch on something else before we move on to the next chapter, LOVE. I know I get a lot of questions about, "Well how can I do all these things" and "why would I do all these things if I don't love the guy". Love is an emotion. It's not a given because you are in a relationship. Sometimes it takes you a few month's to love someone and sometimes it takes years but loving someone or not loving someone doesn't mean you can't be happy in your relationship. So if you're in a relationship with someone that you don't love it's not a big deal. Another thing about love is that it typically occurs at different times for each person in the relationship. Example: the dating process is mostly for women, so odds are women might fall in love first. I say this because the man is giving you his best in the beginning, in an attempt to show that he is worthy or a "good-catch" and most times women will remain reserved. For a man, it may take longer, he may need to gain trust, and he may need to view you as a loyal person and that may take years. So love is a component to a relationship but it doesn't mean success or happiness. There are a lot of people who love each other who can't stand to be around their husband or wife and they're miserable. Again, just because you don't love someone right now doesn't mean that you can't be happy right now. If you're willing to follow the guides in the book and you're with the right guy then love will surely follow.

Man in the Mirror

Men and women are reflections of what they learned through their whole life. If a woman had a mother that was always putting men down and preaching about being independent, most times, that's how those women actions will be. Let's take a man for example. If he learned growing up that women are no good, they are all only after money and its better not to settle down with one, most times, that's how that man's actions will be. Men and women have to have patience with one another. It's all about devising a plan together and learning collectively from your individual growing pains. See people really don't know where their significant other comes from but more importantly, who they come from. We have to recognize the best ways to change those views that are taught and that are embedded into us is by learning and education of one's self. How? Listen to your spouse. Locate where the confusion is coming from and don't have an opinion about everything. We have to remember that people are conditioned to think a certain way until directed otherwise.

Enough is enough

I get posed with the question all of time of "when do you think it's acceptable for a woman to leave the guy she's with? My answers are:

> 1. If he lies, then you should go. There should be zero tolerance for lying in a relationship by a man. In the relationship, women are supposed to lie. They are supposed to be afraid and confused but a man should never display that emotional state since they are the leader. A man should always have open communication and control with his woman no matter how bad the truth may be. As a good leader you must be capable of resolving issues and finding resolution through the truth. With lies, you are attempting to resolve issues based on false premise, which leads relationships on dummy missions. It's a waste of time for all parties involved. Now what woman would want to follow a man like that? Leave him.
> 2. Any physical altercation, no need to elaborate, get out of there.
> 3. If that man can't teach you or you're not learning anything from that man, then it's time to go. You're suppose to improve as a person from relationships and if your relationship isn't doing that for you, then move on. Growth should be the goal for any aspect of your life, especially in your relationship. If you're going to be spending your life with a man who will be leading you, you should make sure it's with a man that can feed

you mentally. Someone that is stimulating and fulfilling those needs. Also on a side note, if you're with someone and you feel like he needs to follow you, for whatever reason, then you're with the wrong person. You should move on, neither one of you will be happy in this situation.

Plain and simple, we make a lot of excuses for people that we're in relationships with but that doesn't mean it is right. If you want to stay in a relationship and be miserable that's totally up to you.

Men also come up to me and ask the same question: When do I know that she's the one or if I should let her go? My answer for men is easy. If she's capable of performing the 4 laws effortlessly, then you have a keeper. If that woman can only do one of the laws, leave her. If that woman can only do two of the laws, leave her. If that woman can do three of the laws though, still, leave her. She should be able to do all four. Because all four means you have a working partner. Where men tend to go wrong is that they make decisions with their eyes. Everyone wants an attractive woman but why suffer for the rest of your life for a few good months or years of sex. If a woman, no matter how attractive she is doesn't believe in your system, you cannot promote or give into them. As said before, guys always want to promote the mailroom workers, janitors or secretary detail to the boss because of looks when they don't have the credentials to do anything other than what they are doing. It's a huge mistake and men pay for it.

Improve Yourself for Yourself

Step 1: Be Honest with Yourself

Self-awareness. You have got to be capable of being fully honest with yourself about your own weaknesses and short comings. Things that you would like to improve about yourself, focus on some of them and accomplish them. If you feel like you aren't interesting enough then open yourself up to new ideas. The more things you know and learn about, the more interesting you become. People like interesting people. Now to be very clear about this you never do this for anyone but yourself, meaning, don't try to learn about football because you think men like football and deep down inside you hate it. Do things because you want to improve yourself. Learn about things that you're interested in. Grow for yourself. As you do these things, you'll notice it also makes you feel more desirable and more attractive. So you have to be able to be honest with yourself about what you want to work on and what things you think are holding you back and dedicate the proper attention to them.

Step 2: Cut Ties

Now many women may be asking themselves at this point," I've recognized that this sounds a lot like me with what's going on in the book, so what can I do, how can I change my situation"? Great question, first thing you need to do is take a look around. Take a look at your friends and the company you keep and ask yourself, do I want to be them. If your answer is "No" then move on. There is no need to have friends lingering around if they're anti-the guy you're with and you're trying to have a successful relationship. How can you improve your situation or yourself and become a positive thinker if every friend you have or even if it's one friend, gives you advice from a single independent woman's perspective? It doesn't matter if that friend is in a relationship either, a relationship doesn't mean happiness or knowledge as most women think. Think about it, the women with the most advice are either single or unhappy. And check this out, the friend that's in a happy relationship or marriage never has that much to say to you about yours. You have to wonder why. It's because she's handling her own business and she doesn't have time to get caught up in yours. That woman doesn't relate to your world nor does she want to but these are the type of women you should be surrounding yourself with. If a successful relationship is your goal then you should approach it as any other goal. You want to surround yourself with people that have made it to where you want to be. You wouldn't surround yourself with people that had nothing but negative things to say or who didn't share the same goals as you in life, would you? For example, you wouldn't enroll in school and surround yourself with a bunch of dropouts that only have bad things to say about college and think that you were going to be successful. You wouldn't do that to yourself while you were giving your all and working hard towards your goals. So why would you let those same people everyday around you when you're attempting to have a successful relationship? See other women without any real guidance or any great experiences with a man tend to have dirty minds and contaminate other women they come into contact with. Remove those people from your life and find the friends that follow the 4 laws in this book.

Step 3: Try Harder

You know in life people are taught to give 110% when it comes to sports, studying, trying to obtain a degree or even going to work. Everybody always gives the advice of "do your best and be your best" and it will eventually pay off. What's funny about this advice is that people say it for everything except for a relationship. No one and not even your parents preach to you to give 110% percent in your relationship. It's always the advice of "why you doing that, yall aint married" or "you're going to listen to him, he's not your daddy" or "why you need to check with him first, let's go girl"! It's time to reprogram yourself and tell yourself you have to work for what you want. The advice that a woman should give or receive is "I know you just started dating this guy a month ago and I see you really like him, give all of yourself to him and do the best you can". With that mindset, you would already be eliminating the thought of mediocrity and you will be mentally ahead of other women. So when your friends and family confront you about why are you doing this and why are you doing that, you will be able to tell them, "this is what I want and I deserve someone who can reciprocate this back to me".

Step 4: Forgive the Forgotten

My advice to a scorn woman from a previous relationship would be to try again. My initial thoughts about that woman would be "Why did you stay that long"? That's the real question women have to think about and answer. With the advice of trying again, I would also advise that they give even more effort their next time around. I would tell them from the beginning to give 110%. Go ahead and give up the ass as well so you can see a man's true colors. If you give up the ass in the beginning and you see he isn't returning calls or he has an excuse of why he hasn't seen you or spent any time with you, right then and there, cut him off. Of course, make sure you're having safe sex but go ahead and get that out the way. At that point you will be able to see a man's true intentions and if they're not good it will save you a lot of time and headache because you will know.

There will be a lot of men that you encounter that are liars and that are deceitful because most men are but I cannot stress enough to keep trying. You have to keep trying like you haven't had a bad relationship. You don't want to be so scorned or so drained that when the "right guy" comes along, you're burnt out then you miss out because you don't care about trying. Remember not to change yourself in those fabricated encounters which you will have. You can't allow people to deter you or allow them to get you off track from what you are attempting to accomplish which in this case will be a successful relationship. The type of thinking you would carry in your career and regular life goals by continuing to try, you should apply to your relationship goals.

Remember BOMO. You burn out, you'll miss out.

In Closing

Deep within, all women want to be dependent upon a man. The key to having a woman become dependent would be a man that she can depend on. One that wouldn't make her feel less than in the relationship once she has relinquished her power. We have to remember that most women do think and feel with other women in mind. We also have to keep in mind that most men are liars. Many women will read this book alone, take various examples away, compare their actions, lives and their relationship against the book and be able to improve things. Those same women with friends will say the book is "offensive and they will never do any of those things for a man", which is a mistake. Many men will read the book alone and admit to being a liar. The same men with friends will just use it as a conversation piece. I'm here to tell you it's your choice. This book is an open letter to men and woman to let each other know how we are failing our relationships and failing each other. You can commit to your relationship and do everything to make your man or woman happy or the both of you can remain miserable and desire other people. It all begins with following the laws for a woman and if the guy you're with isn't man enough to respect you and be honest with you when you're doing your part, leave. That will be the only way you will receive happiness. Men, if that woman you're with cannot do her part and carry out her role as the supporter, leave. Everyone knows when it's time to go. We're talking about your life and happiness people. So hopefully, this will ignite a conversation between men and women, husband and wives, so we can finally reach an understanding of what we need from one another and how we can achieve happiness together. If you weren't able to take anything away from the book, I truly feel sorry for you and I know more than likely you're alone or the person you're with is miserable. Happy Husband, Happy Life!

Thank you and we love you all!

www.ingramcontent.com/pod-product-compliance
Lightning Source LLC
Chambersburg PA
CBHW071744020426
42331CB00008B/2173